Malala

Terry Barber

WOMEN
WHO
INSPIRE

Malala is published by
Grass Roots Press, a division of Literacy Services of Canada Ltd.
www.grassrootsbooks.net

ACKNOWLEDGEMENTS

We acknowledge the financial support of the Government of Canada through the Canada Book Fund (CBF) for our publishing activities.   Canadä

Produced with the assistance of
the Government of Alberta through the
Alberta Multimedia Development Fund.   Albertaɴ

Editor: Dr. Pat Campbell
Image research: Dr. Pat Campbell
Book design: Lara Minja

Library and Archives Canada Cataloguing in Publication

Barber, Terry, date, author
    Malala Yousafzai / Terry Barber.

ISBN 978–1–77153–188–7 (paperback)

1. Yousafzai, Malala, 1997-. 2. Women Nobel Prize winners—
Pakistan—Biography. 3. Women social reformers—Pakistan—Biography.
4. Political activists—Pakistan—Biography. 5. Pakistan—Biography.
6. Readers for new literates. I. Title.

PE1126.N43B36457 2016   428.6'2   C2016–906606–1

Printed in Canada.

Contents

A river runs through Swat.

The Land of Beauty

Swat is a land of beauty. Swat is a land of peace. Swat has mountains. Swat has blue lakes. Swat has green valleys. Swat has a river that runs through the valley. For the people of Swat, 2007 is an ugly year.

Swat is in Pakistan.

In 2007, the Taliban kill more than 1,400 people
in Pakistan.

The Land of Death

By 2007, the **Taliban** control Swat. The Taliban are **strict**. The Taliban **forbid** TV. The Taliban forbid music and dancing. The Taliban forbid books. The Taliban forbid photos. The Taliban forbid people to laugh in public.

The Taliban control Swat from 2007 to 2009.

Barbers cannot cut off men's beards.

The Land of Death

The Taliban want all men to grow beards. The Taliban forbid men to wear suits. The Taliban forbid men to wear ties. The Taliban beat men who do not follow these rules. But the Taliban treat women far worse.

These women are wearing burkas.

The Land of Death

The Taliban believe women must serve men. Women must obey men. Women are forced to stay at home. They cannot work. Women cannot go to the market alone. They must go with a man. Women must wear **burkas.**

Pakistan

Malala Yousafzai is born in Mingora, Pakistan.

Early Years

Malala is born on July 12, 1997.
Luck smiles on Malala. Her parents
are kind. They are free thinkers. Many
parents think a boy is of more value
than a girl. Malala's parents know
a girl has as much value as a boy.

Malala's parents
and brothers.

Malala and her mother, Torpekai.

Early Years

Malala's family does not have much money. But the home is full of love. Malala loves her mother. Her mother teaches Malala to speak the truth. Malala loves her brothers. Malala often fights with her older brother. Still, she loves him.

Malala's mother cannot read or write.

Ziauddin, Malala's father.

Early Years

Malala's father is called Ziauddin. Malala has a special relationship with her father. Her father is her role model. They think in the same way. Her father says, "I will protect your freedom." Malala's father wants her to follow her dreams.

Ziauddin is a school principal.

Malala, age 12, sits beside her trophies.

Early Years

Malala is a good student. She works hard in school. Often, she is the top student in her class. Malala knows education is important. She feels lucky to go to school. Many parents do not send their girls to school.

These men clean up after a school is bombed.

Malala's Peaceful Protest

In 2008, the Taliban start to destroy girls' schools. They blow up more than 400 schools in Swat. Malala's school stays open. Later that year, Malala speaks to the press. Malala **protests** the attacks on girls' schools.

Malala wants women to be equal to men.

After the ban, some girls still go to school.

Malala's Peaceful Protest

In 2009, the Taliban **ban** girls from going to school. Malala writes a **blog** about life as a girl under Taliban rule. She writes about being afraid to go to school. At first, Malala signs the blog with a false name.

Malala writes her blog for the **BBC**.

These women watch TV.

Malala's Peaceful Protest

Malala and her father go on TV.
They believe girls have a right to an
education. Malala says, "All I want is
an education. I am afraid of no one."
Malala wins awards for her work.
She becomes famous.

In 2011, Malala
wins Pakistan's
National Youth
Peace Prize.

The streets are empty after people flee Swat.
July 12, 2009.

Malala's Peaceful Protest

Life under the Taliban is filled with danger. In 2009, Malala and her family **flee** Swat. They return a few months later. Malala decides to take a risk. She signs her blog with her real name. The Taliban now know Malala.

Malala in March 2012.

Malala's Peaceful Protest

Malala asks herself a question:

"If the Taliban come, what should I do?"

"Just take a shoe and hit them,"
she tells herself.

Malala cannot do that. If Malala uses
violence, she will be as bad as the Taliban.

In 2011, the
Taliban leaders
vote to kill Malala.

By 2012, women can go out by themselves.

Malala's Peaceful Protest

By 2012, the Taliban no longer control
Swat. Or so people might think.
Malala knows better. Malala knows
the Taliban are still a threat. Malala
knows her father is in danger. Malala
does not think the Taliban will come
after her.

By 2012, the
Government
of Pakistan
controls Swat.

A Taliban fighter.

Malala is Shot

The Taliban do come. Malala is on a school bus. She rides with other girls. The bus stops. A young man comes on the bus. He holds a gun in his hand. His hand shakes. He asks, "Who is Malala?"

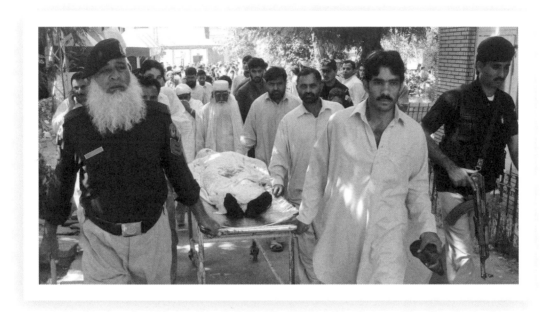

Malala is carried on a stretcher.
October 9, 2012.

Malala is Shot

The man shoots the gun. Malala is hit in the head. Two other girls are shot. Malala can hear the shots. Then, all she remembers is the dark. Malala is taken off the bus. Malala is taken to a hospital.

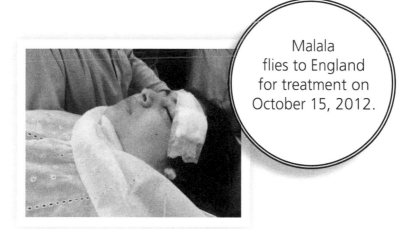

Malala flies to England for treatment on October 15, 2012.

People pray for Malala.

Malala is Shot

The world learns that Malala might die. Malala is shot because she wants an education. Malala is shot because she does not obey the Taliban. The Taliban want Malala dead. Malala lives, but she is not safe.

Malala reads get-well cards at the hospital.

Malala's Smile Returns

Malala heals. The bullet does not cause brain damage. Malala has some nerve damage to her face. Malala cannot smile. Doctors fix the nerve. Malala goes on with her work. By March 2013, Malala is back in school and smiling.

Malala walks to school for the first time after being shot.
March 13, 2013.

Malala's Smile Returns

Malala goes to school in England. She and her family cannot return to Swat. They will be in danger. Malala likes the people in England. Her school is a good school. But Malala misses the beauty of Swat.

Malala wins the Nobel Peace Prize.
December 10, 2014.

Malala's Dreams

Malala wins the Nobel Peace Prize. She is the youngest person to win the prize.

Malala gives a speech. "Let's solve this once and for all," she says. Malala means every child must have the chance to go to school.

Malala dreams about the land of Swat.

Malala's Dreams

Malala has yet to return to Swat.
Swat is a land of danger. Malala
dreams about visiting Swat. Maybe
Swat will become safe again. If Swat
becomes safe, Malala's dream will
come true. She will return home,
to the land of beauty.

Glossary

---

ban: to forbid something with na official order.

BBC: a British TV and radio broadcaster.

blog: a personal website that contains the writer's experiences.

burka: a loose garment that covers the entire body.

flee: to run away from a place of danger.

forbid: to order someone not to do something.

protest: to complain about something.

strict: demanding that rules are obeyed.

Taliban: a political group that holds extreme views.

Talking About the Book

What did you learn about Malala?

What words would you use to describe Malala?

How do you think Malala's parents felt when she signed her blog with her real name?

Why did the young man shoot Malala?

Would you risk your life for education?

How did Malala make the world a better place?

Picture Credits